D1468153

JOHANNES GUTENBERG

Publishing Pioneers

JOHANNES GUTENBERG

PRINTING PRESS INNOVATOR

by Sue Vander Hook

Content Consultant:
Frank Romano
Professor Emeritus, RIT School of Print Media

ABDO
Publishing Company

CREDITS

Published by ABDO Publishing Company, 8000 West 78th Street,
Edina, Minnesota 55439. Copyright © 2010 by Abdo Consulting
Group, Inc. International copyrights reserved in all countries. No
part of this book may be reproduced in any form without written
permission from the publisher. The Essential Library™ is a
trademark and logo of ABDO Publishing Company.

Printed in the United States.

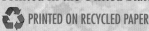 PRINTED ON RECYCLED PAPER

Editor: Jill Sherman
Copy Editor: Rebecca Rowell
Interior Design and Production: Becky Daum
Cover Design: Becky Daum

Library of Congress Cataloging-in-Publication Data
Vander Hook, Sue, 1949-
 Johannes Gutenberg : printing press innovator / by Sue Vander
Hook.
     p. cm. — (Publishing pioneers)
 Includes bibliographical references and index.
 ISBN 978-1-60453-762-8
 1. Gutenberg, Johann, 1397?-1468—Juvenile literature. 2.
Printers—Germany—Biography—Juvenile literature. 3. Printing—
History—Origin and antecedents—Juvenile literature. I. Title.
 Z126.Z7V35 2009
 686.2092—dc22

 [B]

                                2009009991

TABLE OF CONTENTS

Johannes Gutenberg worked in Mainz, Germany.

The Work of the Books

ourt was ready to begin, but the defendant—Johannes Gutenberg—was not there. It was Thursday morning, November 6, 1455. The court of the archbishop was in session at the Convent of the Friars Minor in Mainz, Germany.

If the defendant did not arrive soon, the hearing would proceed without him. Gutenberg had appeared at earlier hearings on the matter of his unpaid debt to Johann Fust, but today, Gutenberg was nowhere to be found.

Fust sent a messenger throughout the monastery to inquire about Gutenberg's whereabouts. No one seemed to know where he was, but three of his friends, including Heinrich Keffer and his son, were in the building and on their way to the courtroom. The men stated that Gutenberg had asked them to come to court and witness the proceedings.

These men planned to wait for the outcome of the case. Then, they would swiftly take the news to Gutenberg, who had decided not to go to court that day. In his workshop, Gutenberg waited anxiously for the decision. He likely paced around his printing press, past rows of molded metal letters, and under the large printed sheets that hung from the ceiling to dry.

An Unpaid Debt

At court, Fust waited impatiently with his family and associates. Several other citizens of Mainz were also there to watch and testify. At about noon,

Fust insisted that the hearing proceed without the defendant.

With quill in hand, the judge began writing down the testimonies:

> *Now Johann Fust has brought the following charges against the aforementioned Johann Gutenberg: firstly, that under the terms of their written contract, he [Fust] was to advance in good faith the sum of 800 golden florins to Johann Gutenberg, with which the latter was to carry out the work . . . and that Johann Gutenberg was to pay him interest at six percent on these 800 guilders.*[1]

The record went on to describe a second loan for another 800 guilders at the same interest rate. The two loans came to a great deal of money—the equivalent of about 25 years' wages for an average German peasant. In order to loan the money to Gutenberg, Fust had taken out a loan for himself.

Now, Fust declared under oath:

"Of all the inventions; of all discoveries in science and art; of all the great results in the wonderful progress of mechanical energy and skill; the printer is the only product of civilization necessary to the existence of free man."[2]
—*Charles Dickens*

> *I, Johannes Fust, have borrowed in my own name 1550 guilders which were then handed over to Johann Gutenberg and which were to be spent on our common undertaking, on which I have paid interest and compound interest,*

some of which is still outstanding to this day. . . . I demand from him the interest due under the terms of the verdict.[3]

Fust had been paying interest on his own debt, but Gutenberg had not paid Fust anything. Now, Fust was demanding payment in full.

In the earlier hearings, Gutenberg had claimed that Fust's loan was for an apparatus that would benefit both of them. They were partners in a secret undertaking. Both men had been careful not to describe the apparatus in court or give away any secret details about Gutenberg's work. They referred to the mysterious equipment as "it," the "enterprise," and "art and invention." Gutenberg had believed that as long as the apparatus was for *das Werck der Bucher*—"the work of the books"—Fust would not demand repayment of the loan.[4] But Gutenberg was mistaken. Fust insisted he pay the entire sum of the loans plus interest. According to the contract, if Gutenberg could not or would not pay, Fust could take the apparatus for himself.

Gutenberg probably stayed at the workshop that day because he knew he was going to lose his battle with Fust. For decades, he had kept his amazing machine—his printing press—a secret. He was waiting to announce the invention until he had perfected it. Now, on the eve of its introduction to the world, Gutenberg was in danger of losing it completely.

THE COURT'S DECISION

As Gutenberg was pondering his future, Keffer and his son burst into his workshop. They announced that the judge had ruled in Fust's favor. Gutenberg had lost the lawsuit. Now, he had to pay his debt. The amount he had to pay was not important. He was broke. He could not pay Fust anything.

In the coming days, Fust took the press along with the paper, the vellum, the ink, the molds, the type, the chase, and the printed pages he and Gutenberg had worked on. Gutenberg even lost most of the people who worked for him.

Fust immediately set up his own printing business. Gutenberg had worked on the printing press for most of his life, but Fust gave him no

Renaissance

Gutenberg lived during an era known as the Renaissance, which means "rebirth." This period saw a great revival in art, literature, science, and education in Europe. The Renaissance, which lasted from the fourteenth century to the mid-seventeenth century, is considered a link between the Middle Ages and the modern era. The period is probably best known for the printing press and artistic achievements of people such as Leonardo da Vinci and Michelangelo. Each artist is an example of the so-called Renaissance man, a well-educated person who has a wide range of interests and expertise.

credit for the machine. Fust displayed his own logo on everything he printed—taking credit for page after page of text that was printed on the press Gutenberg had perfected.

RECOGNITION

Before the printing press, books had been written and copied by hand using a pen made from a quill, or a feather. Copying one book by hand took a scribe one or two months, sometimes years. Johannes Gutenberg's development of the printing press revolutionized society. Yet, he was never recognized during his lifetime

The Gutenberg Museum

In 1900, about 500 years after the estimated birth of Johannes Gutenberg, a group of German citizens founded the Gutenberg Museum in Mainz, Germany. It honored the man who developed the printing press. A replica of Gutenberg's printing press is on display at the museum. The reproduction has traveled the world and been shown at many exhibitions.

In 1925, the museum added a reconstruction of Gutenberg's workshop. There, typesetting and printing were demonstrated. In 1927, the museum moved into the Römischer Kaiser building, one of the most beautiful buildings in Mainz. During World War II, the building was heavily bombed, but Gutenberg's equipment and the printing press were preserved. The contents of the museum had been stored off-site in a safe place.

The building was restored in 1962 on Mainz's two-thousandth anniversary. Since then, the museum has acquired a second Gutenberg Bible, Gutenberg's most famous printing. It has also opened the Print Shop, an educational unit where artists can learn about printmaking. In 2000, on what is believed to be the six-hundredth anniversary of Gutenberg's birth, the museum building was restored, updated, and expanded.

The Most Important Invention

In 1997, *Time-Life* magazine chose Gutenberg's printing press as the most important invention of the second millennium. In 1999, the A&E cable/satellite network ranked Gutenberg first on its "People of the Millennium" countdown.

for his accomplishment. A few years after his death, however, Professor Guillaume Fichet at the University of Paris acknowledged that, indeed, Gutenberg had developed the art of printing. In a December 31, 1470, letter, Fichet wrote:

> *Not far from the city of Mainz, there appeared a certain Johann whose surname was Gutenberg, who, first of all men, devised the art of printing, whereby books are made, not by a reed, as did the ancients, nor with a quill pen, as do we, but with metal letters, and that swiftly, neatly, beautifully. Surely this man is worthy to be loaded with divine honors by all the Muses, all the arts, all the tongues of those who delight in books.[5]*

By 1500, more than 1,000 printing shops had sprung up in Europe. Printers were turning out an average of 500 books per week. No other invention had spread so quickly or had such far-reaching effects. Gutenberg's printing press—his "work of the books"—set in motion a new age of knowledge and information.

Gutenberg is memorialized in Mainz.

Gutenberg was born in Mainz.

Patricians' Child

Johannes Gutenberg was probably born in June, but no one is certain of the year. Historians believe it was between 1394 and 1404. Johannes made an uneventful entrance into the world at the *Hof zum Gutenberg*, the House of

Gutenberg. This was his family's home in Mainz, Germany. His father, Friele Gensfleisch zur Laden, was a merchant. He dealt in the profitable cloth trade, as his father and grandfather had done. In addition, he was a member of the Society of Companions of the Mint. This elite group managed the production of gold coins in the city.

Johannes's mother, Else Wirich, was the daughter of a mere shopkeeper. She was of a lower social status than her husband. She did own property, however. She had inherited a country estate in Eltville, not far from Mainz. Johannes had an older brother named Friele, after his father, and an older sister named Else, after her mother.

Johannes's family was not part of the nobility. They were patricians, ranking among the more than 100 "worthy" families in the city. The status gave Johannes's father the right to trade in cloth, sit on the city council, and not pay taxes. Patricians gave a lump sum of money to the city each year. In return, the city paid the patricians a yearly annuity, which was a return on their investment.

Remains of Gutenberg's Birthplace

Throughout the years, Gutenberg House, where Johannes Gutenberg was born and raised, has been destroyed and rebuilt several times. Eventually, it was completely demolished and replaced with a pharmacy.

The money to pay the patricians came from taxes paid by members of the guilds. Guilds were associations similar to present-day labor unions. They formed according to trade. Guilds for blacksmiths, carpenters, textile workers, shoemakers, goldsmiths, and more were common. Guild members resented patricians. After all, guild members paid taxes yet had no say in city government. And their taxes were used to pay annual sums to the patricians. The struggle between the guilds and the patricians was a constant source of conflict for Johannes and his family.

Johannes was not known by either of his parents' last names. At the time, in Germany, people were known only by their first names—family names did not pass from generation to generation. Several other residents of Mainz were named Johannes, however. A patrician with a common name, such as Johannes,

Guilds and Master Craftsmen

As early as 300 AD, workers formed associations, or guilds, based on their trades. The founder of a guild was usually a master craftsman, the highest professional level after serving as an apprentice and a journeyman. In present-day Germany, a person must still be a *Meister*, or master craftsman, to run certain businesses. Electricians and chimney sweeps, for example, must be *Meisters* educated completely in their craft and with at least three years of hands-on experience as journeymen.

was often identified by the house he lived in. The name of a house stayed with it for centuries, no matter who was living there. Thus, Johannes was often called Johannes zum Gutenberg. Later, he was called simply Johannes Gutenberg. In addition, the spellings of names and other things was not standardized in Gutenberg's time. His name often appears in historical documents under a variety of spellings.

The three-story, two-wing Gutenberg House had small, wood-shuttered windows with no glass. This allowed little light on the first floor, which was used for storage. Several families—Johannes's family and other relatives—lived in the two upper floors, where candles lit the dreary rooms. The family was fortunate to have the candles, though, as only patricians could afford this luxury. The peasants had to manage with the light from their fireplaces, the sole source of heat. Houses at that time had no electricity and no plumbing. Chamber pots were used to collect waste, which was dumped out a window into the street. With any luck, the contents missed passersby and landed in the smelly sewage ditch that ran alongside the road.

EDUCATION AND THE RENAISSANCE

Johannes was probably baptized, according to custom, at St. Christopher's Catholic Church, which was next door to the Gutenberg House. There were many schools in Mainz. Patricians usually sent their children to schools operated by a monastery or a church, while children of guild members typically went to schools run by the townspeople.

At one time, boys who were fortunate enough to receive an education became priests or monks. Girls sometimes joined a convent, where they lived as nuns. But during the early 1400s, Germany and the rest of Europe were experiencing the Renaissance—a rebirth of interest in science, art, and exploration. People were no longer satisfied with only a religious education. They often went against the teachings of the Catholic Church to embrace Greek and

Remains of the Church

St. Christopher's Church was built between 1292 and 1325. It was bombed in 1945, during World War II. The chancel, the area around the altar, is all that remains. It is preserved as both a memorial of the war and the historic cathedral. The baptismal, where Johannes Gutenberg is believed to have been baptized, still stands.

Latin literature or form their own new ideas. Free thinking, originality, exploration, and invention were becoming more acceptable.

The demand for education and books was growing rapidly. However, books were scarce when Johannes was in school. Most likely, the teacher had the only copy of each book used in the classroom. For centuries, scribes had been copying books by hand. They meticulously drew letters and decorated pages with versals and artwork. The time-consuming process resulted in just

Valuable Books

The word *manuscript* literally means "written by hand." Between the fifth century and the mid-fifteenth century, scribes primarily produced scrolls and books by hand. Most scribes were monks working in the secluded cloisters of a monastery. They were shut away from the ordinary world. Scribes spent hours, days, weeks, and months drawing elaborate letters, designs, and art. They painted their work with bright colors and embellished it with strands of gold and silver. The metals sparkled in the light. Thus, scrolls and books came to be called "illuminated manuscripts."

The time and artistry put into one book made it a valuable item. Often, a city or empire treasured one of these precious objects. Books also became items coveted by thieves and were sold on the black market. As a result, libraries set up security measures, such as chaining books to tables and shelves. Anyone who borrowed a book had to leave a security deposit, either money or another book of equal value. The person's valuables would be returned when the borrowed book was. Libraries and universities loaned books to each other without a deposit. While the book was on loan, a scribe often copied it to add to the borrowing library's own collection.

one additional precious copy of a scroll or a book. Scribes mostly copied sacred texts, such as the Bible. They also copied grammar books, wrote down court proceedings, and kept historical records for kings and nobility.

A Lively City

Johannes's education went beyond school. He also learned from his father about goldsmithing and the metalwork that went on at the mint. And he learned a lot just by living in Mainz. This rich, bustling city fed off the lively trade where the Rhine and the Main rivers met. Dozens of merchant ships were usually anchored on the Rhine, the primary trade route through Europe. Cloth trade was the main source of income for the people of Mainz. On any given day, Johannes could have watched tall cranes dangle huge bales of cloth over the docks and swing them onto the shore. Horse-drawn carriages waited there to haul goods through the city's main gate, called the Iron Tower. The goods were carted along the city streets to waiting merchants, craftsmen, and shopkeepers.

Spires towered above the city. These tall steeples held bells that tolled daily to remind people that

A city street in historic Mainz

Mainz was alive and prosperous. Indeed, this flourishing city was famous for its fine cloth and abundance of gold, silver, and skilled goldsmiths. People came from all over to buy fine jewelry, coins, and other items. The city was aptly called *Aurea Moguntia*—"Golden Mainz."

In the center of the city was St. Martin's Cathedral. Its bell tower and spires rose higher than all the rest. Below, crowds of merchants broadcast their wares in the din and confusion of the chaotic city. On the streets and in the shops, people sold anything from fish to flax. They marketed freshly baked breads, shoes, wines, metals, jewelry, imported fabrics, and much more. The sights, smells, noises, and excitement would have made a young boy such as Johannes curious to learn more about his world and the craftsmen who kept the city's economy strong.

But when Johannes was about 13 years old, life as he knew it in Mainz changed drastically. Johannes learned what it was like to be hated, and he found himself in the middle of a political revolt that would alter his life. ⌐

When Gutenberg was growing up in Mainz, St. Martin's Cathedral was newly constructed.

The Gutenberg family probably lived in Eltville after they left their home in Mainz.

A City Divided

It was the summer of 1411 when Johannes Gutenberg and his family were forced to leave Mainz. They packed up their belongings in a horse-drawn carriage and left behind Gutenberg House. Centuries-old clashes between the guilds and the patricians had peaked. Members of the guilds took control of the city. They were revolting against the patricians, who had all the privileges, all the power, and all the money. Revolution had happened before, in 1332, when a civil war caused the patricians to leave town. But the revolution ended when the common citizens could no longer survive without patrician money. Then, the patricians returned to the power and the prosperity they had enjoyed before they left.

In all, 117 patrician families left Mainz in 1411. They found safe places to live in the surrounding countryside. Friele Gensfleisch hastily fled with his wife, Else, and their three children. They most likely went to Else's Eltville estate. There, they waited for the uprising to calm down. But the guilds grew stronger by joining forces. They made greater demands, insisting that patricians return and start paying taxes. They demanded a voice on the city council and a say in how patricians were paid on their investments. The Roman Catholic archbishop, who was both the spiritual leader and the political leader of Mainz, tried to resolve the issues and bring unity back to the city. But the conflict went on for years.

If Johannes did live in Eltville during that time, he may have attended the local school at the Church of St. Peter and Paul. Education was advanced there. The school had classes in Latin and lessons from the Latin grammar book *Ars Grammatica.* The book was commonly called the *Donatus* after its author, Aelius Donatus. The students also studied Virgil, Terence, and other classical Latin authors.

RETURN TO MAINZ

In 1414, when Johannes was in his mid-teens, Friele Gensfleisch returned to Mainz with his family. The disputes between the patricians and the guilds were not over, but the atmosphere was peaceful enough to return. Johannes's father did not go back to serving on the town council, but he did return to his job at the mint.

Johannes most likely studied with his father at the mint, learning

---

Ars Grammatica

Ars grammatica is a general title for textbooks of Latin grammar. A variety of such books have been written by different authors. The first edition of *Ars Grammatica* was written by Aelius Donatus and called *Ars Minor.* It is a brief summary of the eight parts of speech: noun, pronoun, verb, adverb, participle, conjunction, preposition, and interjection. The information is presented as a series of questions. For example, "How many numbers does a noun have?" The expected answer is "two: singular and plural." Another edition, *Ars Major,* is longer and more advanced. It includes topics such as metaphor, allegory, and sarcasm.

metallurgy, the art of creating objects from metals. It combined technology and art. And Mainz had some of the best metal craftsmen around.

A University Education

In addition to learning metallurgy, Johannes probably attended Germany's University of Erfurt around 1418. The university at that time was changing its curriculum. The new course of study mixed the supreme authority of the Catholic Church with new Renaissance teachings and philosophies.

The professor typically stood at a pulpit at the front of a room

Metalwork

Minting coins was a complex and artful task. During his time at the mint, Gutenberg learned the art of metalwork. This included making reliefs, which are designs or pictures that are slightly raised from a surface.

To make coins, a goldsmith had to pour hot molten gold into a mold of that coin. A mold is a shell that surrounds every part of the coin. It contains the exact image that appears on the coin. But the image in the mold is a mirror image of the one that appears on the finished coin. The mold is hollow. The liquid gold is poured into the mold, where it is allowed to cool. Once the gold cools and hardens, the mold can be removed. What remains is a brand-new gold coin.

The art of engraving and mold making was important to Gutenberg's development of the printing press. But instead of using these techniques to make coins, Gutenberg shaped all the letters of the alphabet. And he used these letters to make one more thing: a printed page of type.

One of Gutenberg's earliest projects was printing the Ars Grammatica.

furnished only with wooden benches. He lectured on grammar, logic, physics, philosophy, and psychology. He taught Latin, classical literature, and the principles of the Church. While he read from books, the students themselves had no books.

They simply took notes on what the professor taught them. Johannes's education surely affected his beliefs and his worldview.

In 1419, while Johannes was attending the university, his father died, leaving both a will and a family legacy. Johannes returned to Mainz for a short while that year. But Johannes found that he would not inherit his father's position as a patrician or his right to sell cloth. Johannes was excluded because of his mother's lower status as the daughter of a shopkeeper.

In 1420, Johannes likely returned to the university and graduated. Then, he returned to Mainz once again. His sister, Else, was now married. His brother, Friele, was living in Gutenberg House. Their mother had moved to a smaller house. Johannes, neither a patrician nor a guild member, turned to the mint for a job. His uncle worked

Typesetting: A Black Art

In Germany, setting type was considered an art form. It was sometimes called a "black art," referring to the black ink that stained the printers. For the most part, typesetting has been replaced by computer printers. However, some printers still set type and print the way Johannes Gutenberg did. Every year, in Mainz, Germany, some of these traditional book printers meet for a yearly convention.

there, and Johannes knew two other workers at the mint. The art of goldsmithing that he had learned from his father was now the logical career to which he could turn. Although he did not belong to the goldsmith guild, Johannes was still able to work at the mint because of his father's past associations there.

Meanwhile, political strife was still plaguing Mainz. The same issues prevailed: taxes and no guild representation on the city council. By 1428, the financial condition of the city had deteriorated, and bankruptcy for Mainz was likely. The guilds demanded status as the most powerful governing body. Again, many patricians fled the city and went to live in their country estates. Johannes also decided to leave. But this time, he went to Strasbourg, which was 100 miles (161 km) away. He would live and work there for the next 20 years.

Few Books, Great Value

In 1424, England's Cambridge University library owned only 122 books. These handwritten books were so scarce at the time that each book was equivalent in value to a farm or a vineyard.

The Gutenberg family was forced to leave Mainz in 1428.

During the 1400s, the German middle class wore clothes similar to these.

Mysterious Business

While Johannes Gutenberg was establishing himself in Strasbourg, the guilds were gaining ground back home in Mainz. In 1429, the elections for city council resulted in 28 seats for guild members and only 7 for patricians.

The following year, the archbishop decreed in an act of reconciliation, "We have considered long enough such confusion and discord as are unfortunately now common in the German lands."[1] He went on to say, "Henceforth, the council of Mainz shall have 36 members; of these, 12 shall be of the old families [patricians] and 24 from the community [the guilds]."[2]

Then, the archbishop asked the patricians to return to the city and abide by the reconciliation. But few patricians came back. The city's finances continued to crumble. By 1430, all the former rights of the patricians had been restored to bring money back to the city. The guilds were again forced to give in to the patricians.

LIFE IN STRASBOURG

Gutenberg, however, did not return to Mainz. By this time, he had an idea for a printing press. Strasbourg seemed like a good place for him to work out the details of building his device. Strasbourg was a pleasant place where the River Ill flowed into the Rhine. The guilds had been in charge of that city for nearly a century. Quaint shops lined the streets, and businesses hummed with activity. The ornate

Strasbourg Cathedral towered above all the other churches and buildings. The cathedral's north tower was under construction. Sculptors worked busily every day carving stone in the courtyard.

Gutenberg had found a perfect place to start his project. He also had a family connection to Strasbourg. Gutenberg's brother had a share in the city's government. Once a year, Friele traveled to Strasbourg to collect his annuity.

Threats to the Strasbourg Cathedral

During World War II, the stained glass windows in the Strasbourg Cathedral were removed. They were stored in a salt mine near Heilbronn, Germany, to protect them from being damaged by bombs. After the war, the windows were reinstalled by the U.S. government. Decades later, in 2000, Strasbourg Cathedral was again in danger. That year, German authorities foiled a plot to blow up the historic church.

INHERITANCE ISSUES

In 1433, Gutenberg's mother, Else Wirich, died. She left the two family houses and the Mainz annuity to her three children. The siblings agreed that Else would get Gutenberg House and Friele would have the estate in Eltville. Johannes's share of the inheritance was Friele's Strasbourg annuity and a portion of the Mainz annuity.

Gutenberg was pleased to get the money. It would allow him to stay in Strasbourg and work on his project.

But there was a problem: he had to appear in person in Mainz to collect his money. And because he was not there, the city leaders decided it was not important to save the money for Gutenberg.

Eventually, Gutenberg was able to get a document signed by all three of Mainz's magistrates, in which they personally guaranteed payment to Gutenberg of 310 guilders. However, Gutenberg still did not receive payment. In 1434, he got a chance to collect his money. One of the magistrates, Niklaus von Wörstadt, happened to visit Strasbourg. Gutenberg approached von Wörstadt and demanded

Misunderstandings and Lawsuits

In 1436 and 1437, a woman named Ellewibel filed a lawsuit against Gutenberg. She claimed that he broke his promise to marry her daughter, Ennelin. Ellewibel was convinced Gutenberg was the man for her daughter. She even told her neighbors and relatives that the two would be married. However, it is unlikely that Gutenberg made such a promise.

When Ellewibel tried to set a wedding date, she was told there would be no marriage. Ellewibel was humiliated by the refusal, especially after she had spread news of the betrothal. She persuaded her daughter to sue Gutenberg. She even found a local shoemaker named Klaus Schott to testify on her behalf.

Gutenberg was outraged at the lawsuit. He claimed that he had no intention of marrying Ellewibel's daughter. But, he was especially angry about the lies Schott told in court. During the hearing, Gutenberg called him "a miserable wretch who lives by cheating and lying!"[3] In turn, Schott sued Gutenberg for defamation, and the court made Gutenberg pay Schott damages in the amount of 15 guilders.

payment. The document proved that von Wörstadt owed him the equivalent of five years' salary. Unable to pay the large sum on demand, von Wörstadt was taken to debtor's prison.

The magistrate promised to pay Gutenberg within a few months. Gutenberg believed von Wörstadt and filed a document on March 14, 1434, that released von Wörstadt from prison. Back in Mainz, von Wörstadt arranged for the city to pay Gutenberg his annuity. The magistrate fulfilled his promise, and Gutenberg received his annuity.

A Mysterious Man

Finally, with a sizable amount of money in hand, Gutenberg rented a large house next to the St. Argobast Monastery. It was a little more than one mile (1.6 km) outside Strasbourg on the River Ill. Gutenberg had to do his work outside the city limits because it required a forge to make metals hot enough to mold, shape, and engrave them. An ordinance forbade forges within the city limits because they could cause a fire.

No one was sure what Gutenberg was doing out in the country. No one really even knew who he was. Some documents referred to him as a goldsmith, others as a member of a guild, and still others as belonging to Strasbourg's upper class.

Gutenberg did everything he could to keep his life and his work secret. People he hired to help him—namely, Hans Riffe, Andreas Heilmann, and Andreas Dritzehn—were sworn to secrecy. These local patricians had invested money in Gutenberg's project, so they were motivated to keep quiet. They also helped Gutenberg raise money to keep the project going. Gutenberg's inheritance was dwindling, and he needed more money to buy supplies. He had a great idea for how to get it.

A Plan to Fund the Project

Every seven years, a huge pilgrimage of Roman Catholics made their way to the city of Aachen, about 150 miles (241 km) north of Strasbourg. It was home to the magnificent Aachen Cathedral, the oldest Roman Catholic church in northern Europe. The Royal Church of St. Mary, as it was also called, claimed to have some of the most sacred religious relics in Europe.

No Patents

Today, an inventor can get a patent to protect his or her work. Issued by the government, a patent guarantees that inventors control the rights to their ideas or inventions, so others cannot steal or profit from their work. In the 1400s, there were no patents. An inventor such as Gutenberg had to guard his work with watchful secrecy. He had to trust his friends and employees to maintain confidentiality.

Pilgrimage

Roman Catholics still flock to the city of Aachen, Germany, every seven years to catch a glimpse of the sacred relics stored at Aachen Cathedral. The last pilgrimage took place in June 2007.

These relics included the robe of the Virgin Mary, Jesus's swaddling clothes, Christ's loincloth, and the cloth in which the severed head of John the Baptist had been wrapped. These treasures were taken out of the shrine once every seven years for public viewing.

One glimpse of these sacred relics was said to protect a person from many ills. By the early 1400s, the crowds had become so large that church officials moved the viewing outside the city. They locked the city gates and held up each item from atop a high platform. About 10,000 pilgrims a day during a two-week period could only hope to catch a far-off glimpse of the relics. So, each pilgrim carried a special mirror—a convex piece of shiny metal that captured wide-angle reflections. Pilgrims climbed on top of city walls or to the tops of the highest hills, or they squeezed between buildings. They held up their mirrors, hoping to catch a reflection of one of the sacred items.

Gutenberg's moneymaking idea was to craft and sell these metal mirrors. And what a market he had in 140,000 eager pilgrims! Gutenberg and his three partners met the challenge. By 1439, the year of the next pilgrimage, the men had made enough mirrors and were ready to travel to Aachen. They planned to sell each mirror for about half a guilder (about ten dollars today). That year, however, the bubonic plague—the Black Death—hit Europe. The Aachen pilgrimage was postponed to the following year. There was no market for the mirrors that year, and the men took a huge loss.

Riffe decided to end his association with the group. Dritzehn got sick with the plague and died. Then, Gutenberg found himself in court being sued by Dritzehn's brothers. They wanted to recoup their brother's losses from the mirrors. They also wanted to claim their right to inherit Dritzehn's partnership with Gutenberg. Dritzehn's brothers knew that Gutenberg was working on something out of the ordinary. They believed the invention would be worth a lot of money.

They also had pieces of the equipment—cutting instruments, forms, and a press—at Dritzehn's house. Gutenberg wanted them back. He tried twice to find the pieces. He believed Dritzehn had left these pieces in a press. In the court hearing, one witness relayed how Gutenberg had instructed one of Dritzehn's brothers to keep the press a secret. Gutenberg had other instructions for the brother:

> He should undo both screws so that the pieces fell apart. He should lay these separate pieces on the press, as nobody would then be able to see or work out what they were for.[4]

Another witness testified about what would happen to the partnership if one partner died:

> If one of them [the four partners] should die during this period then his investment, all things finished or unfinished, . . . should pass to the surviving partners, and the heirs of the deceased should only be entitled to receive back 100 guilders at the conclusion of the enterprise.[5]

Perhaps the hearing revealed a little more than Gutenberg wanted to be made public. But at least he won the lawsuit. The court abided by the agreement the four men had made. In December 1439, the court ordered Gutenberg to pay the Dritzehn brothers 100 guilders. The rest of the money could be used for Gutenberg's "adventure," his "common work," his "secret art," as he called it. The Dritzehn brothers would not become Gutenberg's partners in the venture. Gutenberg's secret was safe—for now.

Johannes Gutenberg moved to Strasbourg, which today is part of France.

Metallic letters were used in printing.

THE PRINTING PRESS

f the bits and pieces of Johannes
Gutenberg's life in Strasbourg could be
pieced together, they would probably tell the whole
story of the printing press. But most of Gutenberg's
work was done in secrecy. Though there are few

records to show it, Gutenberg probably completed his printing press while he was in Strasbourg.

To ensure the project's secrecy, Gutenberg had his operation spread out among several houses. The operation included many functions. Andreas Dritzehn probably did the printing before he died. After all, he had a press of some kind at his house. He also had a cutting instrument, which could have been used to make pieces of type. Andreas Heilmann also had equipment at his house. And Gutenberg had hired an engraver, Hanns Dünne, who could have etched letters to be used in making molds. Many other people worked for Gutenberg, including a goldsmith.

Strasbourg's records show that Gutenberg took out loans while he was there. These loans were large enough to fund a substantial business. And printed copies of the *Donatus* have been found in Strasbourg. If Gutenberg had completed his printing press when he was in Strasbourg, perhaps he printed the *Donatus* while he was there.

Gutenberg would not have wanted to publicize the completion of his printing press until he had made a profit on it. Once others learned of the machine, they would copy it. Then Gutenberg would have to contend with them for jobs to publish various books. If his press was completed in Strasbourg, Gutenberg did not let many people know about it.

Then, in 1444, Gutenberg left Strasbourg. The city was facing imminent war. But Mainz was also in political upheaval. For the next four years, Gutenberg seemed to vanish— no one knows where he went. But, in 1448, he was back in Mainz, where he had first learned to make gold coins at the mint. It was where he had learned the technology that he had adapted for use in printing. Now, he would culminate his project

Gutenberg's Lost Years

For the most part, Gutenberg's life in Strasbourg is a mystery. There is little documentation of what he was doing during this period. However, some of his activities can be pieced together using information in court documents, contracts, and receipts for purchases. In 1436, Gutenberg paid a goldsmith named Hanns Dünne the large sum of 100 florins in exchange for *"das zu dem Drucken gehoret"*—"things to do with printing."[1]

Also, a contract between Gutenberg and Andreas Dritzehn reveals that Gutenberg agreed to show Dritzehn a procedure for polishing precious stones. An agreement with Hans Riffe, Dritzehn, and a goldsmith named Andreas Heilmann dealt with a new procedure for making mirrors to be sold at the Aachen fair. Dritzehn's brothers later sued Gutenberg for their brother's share in the partnership. A court document from this legal hearing reveals that the mirrors were designed to attach to pilgrims' headgear. Pilgrims believed they could capture the image of a holy object in these mirrors.

These documents provide scholars and biographers with a glimpse into Gutenberg's life during his years in Strasbourg.

there. By this time, Gutenberg had perfected his printing press. He would set up his press in his hometown.

By the time Gutenberg returned to Mainz, his sister, Else, had died. Gutenberg House was either empty or inhabited only by Else's husband. Gutenberg moved into the house and set up his printing operation there.

The First Printing Press

Conrad Saspach built the first printing press for Gutenberg in 1436. Saspach followed Gutenberg's design. He made the press of wood using two upright pieces of lumber and cross pieces. In the center was the bed, which held the type. A platen, or flat top piece, moved down onto the type when a wooden screw was turned.

GUTENBERG'S PRESS

Gutenberg's press was made of wood. It looked like a long table that fit beneath a freestanding cabinet or door frame. The long table was used to prepare the paper and ink for pressing. Once everything was ready, the paper, ink, and type were slid under the upright frame of the press. The frame contained the press, which was lowered onto the metal type, paper, and ink, creating a printed page.

Printing was a painstaking, multistep process. First, the type had to be created. These were hard blocks of metal with raised letters at one end. Then, the type had to be arranged into words and

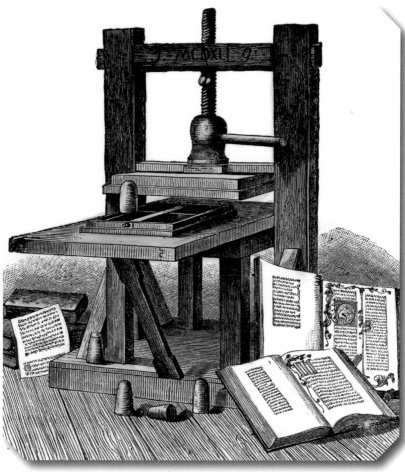

Gutenberg's printing press

sentences. In the final stages, Gutenberg smeared ink on the type and pressed down on the paper. If everything had gone just right, he had successfully printed a document.

A metal punch represented the beginning of each letter to be printed. A punch was a shaft of metal with a tiny raised engraving at one end. There was a punch for every letter of the alphabet in uppercase and lowercase, and for every symbol and punctuation mark. Each letter or symbol was a mirror image of what would be printed on the page.

The first step in printing was to make a matrix. This was a metal mold of a letter that would be used to mold type. To make the matrix, Gutenberg placed a punch, letter side down, on a blank piece of heated metal. He then struck the upper end of the punch with a hammer. That made an indentation of the letter in the metal, in the correct direction. The punch had to be struck just right so every indentation in every matrix had the same depth. It had to be perfect, since it was the master form.

The next step was to make type. To do this, the matrix was placed in the bottom of a small mold. Into the top of the mold, Gutenberg poured molten metal. When it cooled, one piece of type was ready. Many copies

Letters in Relief

A matrix is something from which something else originates or takes form. In printing, the matrix is the mold from which a type—a letter in relief—is formed. It can also refer to the soil or rock in which a fossil is imbedded or the impression of a phonograph record used for mass-producing copies of the original. The word *matrix* comes from the Latin word for "mother" or "mothering agent."

of the same letter were made from the matrix—as many as might be needed on one page of printed text. If the letter *e* appeared 100 times on one page, then Gutenberg needed 100 metal blocks with the letter *e*. When all the characters—the letters, the symbols, and the numbers—were made over and over, they were arranged into words and sentences. Some blocks did not have a letter or a symbol on them. They were intentionally blank and used to make spaces between words.

The next step was gathering the metal blocks together in a frame. The frame held a full page of type snugly in place. This was a very important step because the type had to fit together without gaps, and the surface had to be perfectly level. Each block of type had to be held at exactly the same height. Once the type was set in the frame, it was placed inside a rectangular metal casing called a chase. The chase secured the outside of the frame to hold the page of type tightly in place. If the type moved, the printed letters would smear.

A page of type was now ready for the printing press, but there were still two important elements: ink and paper. Gutenberg made his own ink, a mixture of linseed oil, soot, and amber.

He experimented time and again with various combinations of these ingredients until he created an ink that dried neither too quickly nor too slowly. It also had to be the perfect thickness so it would neither run nor clump. For colored ink, he ground and added the rare lapis lazuli mineral for blue, cinnabar for red, and so forth.

Gutenberg also had to find the right kind of paper. After experimenting repeatedly, he found that the paper had to be somewhat damp so the metal type would make a slight indentation in it. But if the paper was too wet, the ink would dissolve.

Finally, Gutenberg was ready to print a page. He spread ink over the raised letters of type, which appeared upside down and backward. Then, he placed a piece of damp paper carefully on the platen, a flat metal plate attached to the printing press. He then lowered the press.

After the press was lowered, Gutenberg turned a huge screw at the top, forcing down the platen squarely onto the frame. The press pushed the

Presses

Presses had been around for centuries before Gutenberg's printing press. They were used to squeeze juice from grapes and oil from olives. But Gutenberg's printing press was more precise. It could not press the platen down too hard or shift it from side to side. If it did, the ink would smear on the paper.

platen down onto the letters in the frame with just
the right amount of pressure. Too much pressure
would push ink into the little holes of letters such
as *e* and *o*. Not enough pressure would leave gaps in
the straight lines of print. Then, the press was gently
lifted and the paper was hung to dry.

Gutenberg's shop was a busy place, with many
workers setting type, spreading ink, dampening
paper, turning the press, and hanging up pages.
When all the copies of one page were printed and
hung, the process started over.

Gutenberg was not the first person to produce a
printed page. But his method was the most precise
and the most successful of anything tried thus far.
Even the idea of movable type was not completely
unique to Gutenberg. But he was able to use a
language—Latin—that adapted well to his speedy
method of reusing and moving around tiny blocks
of type.

The History of Printing

Through the centuries, other people had
developed ways to print text on scrolls. The Chinese,
the Japanese, and the Koreans had mastered the art
of printing hundreds of years before Gutenberg.

They spread ink on blocks of wood or stone on which they had carved symbols and images. Then, they pressed the inked blocks onto a scroll.

In 770, nearly 700 years before Gutenberg perfected his printing process, the Japanese were printing countless copies of scrolls. But their printing method was not fast. Each block could only be used to print the same set of text over and over. A new block had to be made for each page.

In the eleventh century, Pi-Cheng in China improved the process by making individual characters out of a fire-hardened mixture of clay and glue. The characters were arranged and rearranged into text in a frame, an early form of movable type. He coated them with ink and then imprinted the characters onto a piece of paper or cloth. But there were too many Chinese characters—tens of thousands of them. The process was not practical. The Chinese system of writing was too complex for printing with movable type.

Printed Prayer Scrolls

To celebrate the end of a civil war, Japanese Empress Shotoku ordered 1 million copies of a tiny prayer scroll to be printed, rolled up, and placed inside miniature wooden pagodas that were distributed to every citizen. The project was completed in 770. Shotoku believed the repetition of a prayer held power. These tiny prayer scrolls are believed to be the world's first texts printed on paper. Many of the tiny scrolls still exist today.

In the early 1200s, the Koreans also devised a system of printing using movable type. But the Korean language had 40,000 characters. Copying text by hand was actually faster than putting together type for such a complicated language. The Mongols, the Egyptians, the Greeks, the French, and the Dutch also worked on printing. But none perfected a method similar to Gutenberg's, by which pages of printed text could be reproduced with speed and precision.

Though people tried for centuries to perfect the printing process, it was Gutenberg who successfully developed an efficient method. Now, he put his printing press to work. Gutenberg needed to print a book that would be a popular seller and provide him with income. ⌒

Chinese printers made wooden blocks to print a single page.

Saint Jerome translated the Bible into Latin.

CATHOLIC CONNECTION

ardinal Nicholas of Cusa was worried about the Catholic Church. Nearly every priest was teaching a different theology. Also, practically every copy of the Latin translation of the Bible, or the Vulgate, was different. Whenever a scribe copied the Bible, he made mistakes. And sometimes, he changed the text to agree with his own personal beliefs. If a scribe did not like what the Bible said, he could change it.

A Standard Version

Missals, or the books used to celebrate Mass throughout the year, were also diverse. There was no standard version. Choir books and breviaries, which contained prayers, hymns, and readings, also varied. Nicholas had ordered a group of monks to work on a standard version of the missal. In the late 1440s, the cardinal had to travel to Mainz to approve it. He also wanted the monks to create a standard choir book and breviary. But Nicholas faced strong opposition to his attempts to standardize liturgical books.

Nicholas wanted every church and monastery to have the same copy of the Bible—one accurate version. Then, every priest and monk would be teaching the same theology. Some people were also in favor of making the Bible available to common people. This was a suggestion that raised eyebrows among the clergy, however. A Bible in the hands of ordinary people could take authority away from the Church and the priests.

Gutenberg learned about Nicholas's campaign to standardize liturgical texts. He knew that if he printed a Bible, it would have to be a version that was approved by the Catholic Church, particularly Cardinal Nicholas and Pope Nicholas V.

The Vulgate

The Vulgate is the official Roman Catholic version of the Bible, translated into Latin from the original Hebrew and Greek. *Vulgate* comes from a Latin word meaning "common" or "popular." In the late fourth and early fifth centuries, Pope Damasus I commissioned Saint Jerome to do the translation. Jerome also wrote an introduction to each book of the Bible. In addition, the Vulgate differs from the original Hebrew and Greek texts in other ways. The names of some of the books differ, as do the division of chapters and verses.

Through the years, priests and monks who worked as scribes made handwritten copies of the Vulgate. They formed attractive letters and decorated the margins with elaborate artwork. The beautifully bound Bibles were displayed in churches, monasteries, and convents.

Scribes sometimes made errors or changed the Bible as they copied it. This resulted in a variety of versions with conflicting text. It was the job of the priests to read and interpret the Bible to their parishioners. As a result, various theologies were being taught according to which version of the Bible a priest used.

Hundreds of copies of the Bible would have to be printed. If the holy book was affordable, Gutenberg could sell it to every church, monastery, and school. Then, perhaps each of these institutions would not have to rely on only one precious handwritten copy, which had to be protected from thievery. Maybe every monk, nun, priest, and professor could have his or her own copy of the Bible. And perhaps one day, each parishoner could also own a copy.

A Fledgling Business

Gutenberg may have started making plans for a printed Bible. But he would have to wait until he knew which version of the Bible would be approved by the cardinal and the pope. He also first had to raise money for the undertaking. There would be no printing business unless he had enough money to hire workers and buy paper, ink, and metals.

Though Gutenberg's printing press was working well, it was not bringing in much income. In 1448, he was living off a loan from his cousin, Arnold Gelthus, of 150 guilders. That money was almost gone. For financial reasons, Gutenberg formed a partnership with Johann Fust, a goldsmith who understood the technology of printing. Fust also was a merchant who could recognize the value of printed books. He was willing to invest money in Gutenberg's project.

In 1449, Fust and Gutenberg agreed to become business partners. Fust lent Gutenberg 800 guilders (about $150,000 today), and Gutenberg agreed to

Scribes would elaborately decorate several pages in the Bible.

pay him back at 6 percent interest. The five-year loan was secured with Gutenberg's equipment. If Gutenberg did not repay Fust in five years, Fust could take the printing press and equipment as payment of the loan.

With money in hand, Gutenberg put his printing press to work. For his first project, he chose a sure thing, a sensible book used by every schoolchild. He would print copies of the 28-page *Donatus*. And he would guarantee an error-free edition of a book that each child could have.

The print shop at Gutenberg House now came to life with activity. A calligrapher drew heavy Gothic Latin letters to closely match the look of the handwritten versions. Another worker made a punch and a matrix for every letter and punctuation mark. Metal blocks of type were molded, hardened, and arranged tightly into a frame and a chase. By 1450, the *Donatus* was finished. It sold well, but it was a small project. Gutenberg needed more business.

WORK WITH THE CHURCH

In 1451, Cardinal Nicholas began a tour of Germany and again visited Mainz. His mission was to once more try to convince religious leaders to standardize liturgical books. His idea had met with opposition for some time. Religious men did not want to give up their favorite versions of the Bible or

**Cardinal Nicholas
of Cusa**

Nicholas of Cusa was
born in Kues, now Ger-
many, in the early 1400s.
He chose to spend his life
serving the Roman Catho-
lic Church. In 1449, Pope
Nicholas V appointed
him cardinal, a ranking in
the Catholic Church just
below the pope. Nicholas
of Cusa was an intelligent
theologian, scholar, and
political leader. He wrote
approximately 40 works,
mostly on philosophy,
mathematics, theology,
logic, and infinity. One
of his most famous books
is *On Learned Ignorance*,
written in 1440. His other
books include *Dialogue
on the Hidden God*, *On
Seeking God*, and *On the
Summit of Contempla-
tion*. He believed that true
wisdom lies in recogniz-
ing human ignorance.

prayer book. It seemed an impossible
feat to get 17,000 priests and 350
religious institutions to agree on
one version. But the pope himself
had ordered standardization, and
Nicholas intended to follow through.
The pope told Nicholas that he
"could raise an army and *go to war*, if
that was what it took to get his way."[1]

Gutenberg and Nicholas may have
met in 1451 to discuss how Gutenberg
could print standard texts for the
church. Gutenberg began making the
necessary type to print a missal. His
business would be in good shape if
he had a contract to print hundreds
of books and possibly Bibles with the
support of the pope.

Many people believe that
Gutenberg's motive behind printing
Bibles was not merely financial; it was
also spiritual. He had a great passion
to print the Bible for the masses so
he could "give wings to truth."[2] It
has been said that Gutenberg saw

an eternal purpose in his printing press and in his great undertaking—a way to spread God's word, "scatter the darkness of ignorance, and cause a light heretofore unknown to shine amongst men."[3]

While Gutenberg waited for the right time to print the Bible, he turned to another print job that had to be done quickly. The Catholic Church needed money, and a campaign to sell indulgences began. An indulgence was a document that offered forgiveness of sins if a person did some sort of good work and paid money for the indulgence. Sins could be forgiven for a month or two, depending on the number of good works and the price of the indulgence.

In May 1452, Cardinal Nicholas ordered priests to sell 2,000 indulgences in Frankfurt, Germany, that month. Gutenberg got the job of printing indulgences. The project was successful, and he made some money. But now Gutenberg turned to his biggest venture yet—a printed standard version of the Latin Bible. For such a large project, he would

Missal

The missal, which is Latin for "Mass book," is sometimes called an altar missal. The book contains all the texts of the Mass and is used only by priests. The hand missal, or missalette, is used by people assisting at Mass. After U.S. President John F. Kennedy was assassinated in 1963, Lyndon B. Johnson was sworn in as president of the United States aboard *Air Force One* using a missal that had belonged to Kennedy.

Indulgences

In special circumstances, with the pope's approval, a person could purchase a plenary indulgence—one that forgave all of his or her sins forever. A plenary indulgence cost four or five guilders. People could even purchase indulgences for relatives who had already died. The indulgence would shorten their time in purgatory, a place where the Catholic Church believes people suffer for their sins after they die until they are permitted to enter heaven. With indulgences, everyone was happy in the end—the church added money to its treasury, and the people were absolved of their sins.

need another workshop with more equipment and more workers. Of course, that meant he needed more money. He turned to Fust, who had not yet received payment on the first loan. But Fust must have seen the huge potential in Gutenberg's idea. He lent him another 800 guilders. Their agreement stated that it was for the "work to their common profit" or for the "work of the books."[4]

At the end of 1452, with a new supply of cash, Gutenberg began the project. It would be the most massive undertaking of his life.

Gutenberg examines a page from his printing press.

Gutenberg began printing the Bible in Mainz.

THE GUTENBERG BIBLE

For a printing project as large as the Bible, Johannes Gutenberg needed a place to expand his workshop. He set up a bigger shop in nearby Humbrecht House.

PRINTING THE GUTENBERG BIBLE

Gutenberg hired more workers and purchased more equipment, including six new printing presses. They were probably built by a carpenter named Conrad Saspach. He had left Strasbourg and come to Mainz about the same time as Gutenberg. Gutenberg also bought more metals, ingredients for ink, vellum, and lots of paper. The paper, which came from Italy, was shipped down the Rhine River to Mainz. Vellum, made from animal skins, took longer to get. The skins first had to be cleaned and then stretched and scraped to a very thin texture. Gutenberg decided to print a limited number of Bibles on vellum, since it was expensive. Perhaps the Church would buy these costly copies for the pope and the cardinals.

Next, Gutenberg's craftsmen began making a new style of type. The beautiful letters were designed by calligraphers to match the handwritten work of the scribes in the Bible Gutenberg used as a model. Then, the engravers chiseled the letters into metal. They were large

Vellum Copies of the Bible

Gutenberg printed 30 to 35 vellum copies of the Bible. These copies required about 5,000 calfskins that were shaved, treated, stretched, dried, and scraped. Each skin took a month or more to prepare. Today, 11 full copies of the Gutenberg Bible with vellum pages remain as well as one containing only the New Testament.

enough so the text could be easily read from a pulpit, but they were also small enough to fit well on the page, where 42 lines of text would be lined up in two vertical columns.

At least 292 different blocks of type were eventually made—capital letters, lower-case letters, and punctuation marks. Also, alternative letters that were narrower or wider were made. For example, the letter *I* came in six versions. This was so some words could be squeezed or stretched to make the lines of text the same length.

The Model Bible

Historians are not sure which handwritten version of the Vulgate, the Latin version of the Bible, Gutenberg used as a model for his printed Bible. It would have been one approved by the pope. It also had to be mostly error free and in line with Catholic theology. It probably was one of the most beautiful manuscripts a scribe had ever copied.

Perhaps Cardinal Nicholas of Cusa retrieved an approved Bible from a monastery or a church and lent it to Gutenberg. Compositors would have looked at the model and then set up the type in a frame to match the original page.

The Giant Bible of Mainz faces the Gutenberg Bible in a display at the Library of Congress in Washington DC. The Giant Bible of Mainz is one of the last of the handwritten Bibles, embellished with illuminated text and artwork. It represents the culmination of hundreds of years of copying text by hand and the end of the Middle Ages. The Gutenberg Bible marks the beginning of printing and symbolizes the explosion of learning and knowledge ushered in by the Renaissance. The Giant Bible of Mainz closely resembles the text and layout of the Gutenberg Bible. It may have been the model for Gutenberg's Bible.

A total of 46,000 pieces of type were made. This allowed four to six compositors to work at once. These workers were responsible for arranging the type. They looked at the original text and then set the type in a frame to match the original. It was a tricky job because the type was in mirror image. Compositors had to look at letters, words, and sentences that were turned around and backward, and then they had to read it from right to left.

Then, Gutenberg prepared the black ink. The mixture would cling to the paper or vellum and remain brilliant for centuries to come. He also prepared ink in the richest colors of the rainbow that artists would use for versals. These large, decorative capital letters introduced a section or a book of the Bible. Colored ink would also be used for the artwork that wound around the outer edges of some of the pages and between the columns. Most of these designs looked like vines and leaves. Occasionally, monkeys or birds peeked out from the foliage.

Before the presses could start printing, the paper or the vellum had to be dampened. One sheet of paper was dipped in a bath of water and then placed on top of about five dry sheets. This wetting and stacking process was repeated to form a huge pile

The 42-line Bible

The Gutenberg Bible is called the 42-line Bible, but not every page has 42 lines. When Gutenberg began printing, each page had 40 lines. To save paper, he went up to 42 lines per page. Thus, the first pages printed—pages 1 to 9 and 256 to 265—had 40 lines each. Page 10 had 41 lines. Then, the 42-line pages began on page 11. The spacing between the lines changed, but the margins stayed the same.

of papers. In a few days, a uniform dampness had seeped into all the sheets in the pile. Now, the paper was ready for the ink and the presses. A worker poked small holes in the paper. These would serve as guides for placing it on the platen.

Two men worked at each of the six presses. The inker applied the ink to the surface of the type with a large, soft, round leather ball with a handle on top. The pressman lined up the holes in the sheets of paper and placed them on the platen. Then, he operated the huge screw that lowered the platen and pressed it against the inked type.

Also, each sheet of paper went through the printer four times. On each large sheet of paper was printed four pages of the book: two pages were on the front of the sheet, and two pages were on the back. Each page was printed separately, requiring four printings. The large sheets of paper were grouped by fives. The sheets were folded once and inserted inside each other to make a 20-page section. Pages were not printed in the order they would appear in the book. Printing the correct text on the correct portion and side of the paper was a difficult task.

When the presses were running, at least 20 men labored in Gutenberg's workshop. After about two years, approximately 175 copies of the two-volume Bible were completed. Each Bible contained 1,275 pages. It was not simply a book—it has been described as a masterpiece of "sublime beauty and mastery."[1] Albert Kapr, a modern-day typographer and book designer, described the Gutenberg Bible:

> *For regularity of setting, uniform silky blackness of impression, harmony of layout and many other respects, it is magisterial in a way to which we can rarely aspire under modern conditions.*[2]

PRAISE FOR THE PRINTED BIBLE

The pages of Gutenberg's Bible had been completed in 1455. Even before the Bibles were bound, priests were talking about purchasing the finished books. The 20-page sections of the Bible may have already been for sale as early as 1454. Bishop Enea Silvio Piccolomini caught a glimpse of a section while he was visiting Frankfurt. In a letter

A typesetter arranges letters by hand.

dated March 12, 1455, he excitedly told Spanish Cardinal Juan de Carvajal:

> *Everything that has been written to me about that remarkable man . . . is quite true. I did not see complete Bibles but sections in fives of various books thereof, the text of which was absolutely free from error and printed with extreme elegance and accuracy. Your Eminence would have read them with no difficulty and without the aid of spectacles.* [3]

It is unclear whether the "remarkable man" Piccolomini referred to was Gutenberg or Fust, however. The bishop went on to say that he would try to buy the cardinal a complete Bible when one was ready and that "there have been ready buyers for the volumes, even before they are finished."[4]

LOSING THE WORK

Indeed, Gutenberg's Bible was causing quite a sensation. And then, just as the Bible was about to take the world by storm, Fust sued Gutenberg. Their five-year contract had expired, and Fust demanded the money he had loaned Gutenberg, plus 6 percent interest. But Fust knew Gutenberg did not have any money. Everything was tied up in the "work of the books." After several court hearings, the final hearing was set for November 6, 1455. Fust waited for Gutenberg to appear at the Convent of the Friars Minor, but Gutenberg did not come. Gutenberg knew he had no legal argument. He realized he had made a huge mistake when he had agreed to the terms of Fust's loan.

Why would Fust, on the eve of such a great accomplishment, suddenly demand payment from his partner? Why not wait until the business started

making profits, when Gutenberg would be able to
repay the loan? Many people believe Fust saw how
successful the Bible was going to be and decided
that he no longer needed Gutenberg's help. If Fust
sued Gutenberg for the press and the equipment, he
would receive all the profits from the business and
not have to share them with Gutenberg.

Gutenberg had defaulted on the loan. Fust had
every legal right to demand full payment as well as
interest. He knew Gutenberg could not pay him,
and he went after the equipment. He also wanted the
175 copies of the Bible that were ready to be bound.
As soon as the court hearing ended, all the items in
Gutenberg's workshop belonged to Fust. He even
took most of Gutenberg's workers.

Fust and Gutenberg must have made some deal,
however, about the small print shop at Gutenberg
House. Gutenberg kept the one press and all the
equipment at that location. Fust took the larger
operation, along with the 42-line Bible, which is
another name for Gutenberg's work. Gutenberg was
left with a very small workshop and only memories of
his masterpiece. ⌐

A page of the Gutenberg Bible

A replica of one of the volumes of the Gutenberg Bible

STARTING OVER

ohann Fust wasted no time setting up a printing business of his own and staffing it with most of Johannes Gutenberg's apprentices. Peter Schöffer, who had worked so closely with Gutenberg, became Fust's partner and most valued employee. Going with Fust was a natural move for Schöffer, since his connections with the man ran deep. Fust had adopted Schöffer when he had experienced hard times as a teenager. Fust paid for his university education and training. Fust had probably also gotten Schöffer the job with Gutenberg. Schöffer would later marry Fust's only daughter and become his son-in-law.

But for now, Fust and Schöffer seized their opportunity. They went to work putting together the 175 copies of the Bible. Then, they printed more, all on Gutenberg's presses. Next, they began marketing printed copies of the Bible to the Catholic Church. By 1457, the Bible was for sale and in great demand. Fust and Schöffer took full credit for the first printed version of the Bible. Their fame spread throughout Europe.

Fust and Schöffer also printed and sold other religious texts, such as the *Mainz Psalter*, a Latin translation of the Psalms. It included songs of praise, prayers, and poems. Fust and Schöffer made some advancements in Gutenberg's process as well. They printed the *Psalter* using three different colored inks. Gutenberg had only used up to two colors on some of his pages.

Fame and Printing

At the end of the book, Fust and Schöffer placed a colophon, their printer's emblem. With the logo was a statement in which they not only took credit for the *Psalter*, but also declared they had invented printing. They stated:

> *The present copy of the Psalms . . . was so fashioned thanks to the ingenious discovery of imprinting and forming letters without any use of a pen and completed with diligence to the glory of God by Johann Fust, citizen of Mainz, and Peter Schöffer of Gernsheim, in the year of our Lord 1457.*[1]

In the years that followed, some scholars tried to correct the error and credit Gutenberg with the art of printing. In 1505, Johann Schöffer, oldest son of Peter Schöffer, acknowledged:

> *The admirable art of Typography was invented at [Mainz] in the year 1450, by John Gutenberg, and afterwards improved and perfected by the study, perseverance and labour of John [Fust] and Peter [Schöffer]."*[2]

But ten years later, in a 1515 edition of the *Annales*, Johann Schöffer credited Fust and his father with the invention of printing. He also gave his father and Fust credit for the eventual spread of printing throughout the world:

*Both, Johann Fust and Peter Schöffer,
kept this art secret, and bound all their
workmen, and members of their house,
by an oath not to make it known in any
way. Which art, however, was spread,
in 1462, by these workmen, in divers
countries, and increased.*[3]

PRINTING SPREADS

Despite their faults, Johann
Fust and Peter Schöffer were good
printers who furthered the art
and continued Gutenberg's work.
They were also pioneers in colored
printing. Most of the books they
printed were works the Catholic
Church and the monasteries needed.
Just as Gutenberg had expected,
the Church reformed its theology
and standardized its texts. But now,
Fust and Schöffer were the ones who
benefitted. They produced, among
other books, a Mass book, elaborate
psalters, and a guide to the Catholic

Fust and Schöffer

Johann Fust died of the plague in 1466, 11 years after he won the lawsuit against Gutenberg. His partner, Peter Schöffer, carried on the printing business for 40 more years. He died in 1503, wealthy and respected. His descendants continued the printing trade for two more generations.

Peter's son, Johann Schöffer, took over the business from 1503 to 1531. Although he was a capable printer, he was not classified with the best of his time. Another son, Peter, worked as a die cutter and printer in the German cities of Mainz, Worms, and Strasbourg, as well as in Venice, Italy. In Worms, in 1526, he printed the first English New Testament, which was translated by William Tyndale. The younger Peter's son, Ivo, carried on the printing business in Mainz from 1531 to 1555.

liturgy. Schöffer, a fine calligrapher, produced some high-quality nonreligious books. These included Cicero's *De Officiis* and the *Herbarius Latinus*, an encyclopedia of plants and medicines found in apothecaries. The books printed by both Fust and Schöffer matched the high level of excellence Gutenberg had cultivated.

The people Gutenberg had trained were now starting their own printing businesses all over Europe. Some stayed in Mainz, while others spread out. The first to establish a printing business outside Mainz was Heinrich Eggestein. He had most likely worked for Gutenberg and helped print the 42-line Bible.

People were also coming to Mainz to learn how to print. In 1458, France's King Charles VII sent Nicholas Jenson to Mainz to learn the art of printing. Some believe Jenson learned from Gutenberg. The king planned to bring Jenson back to France with the skills to set up a print shop, but Jenson never returned. The political climate in France had changed considerably by the time he was trained and ready to return.

The Work Continues

Gutenberg continued to print, although on a much smaller scale than Fust and Schöffer. He started over with his one remaining printing press at Gutenberg House. Although he had lost most of his equipment and workers, he continued his "work of the books."

Most likely, his two trusted associates—Heinrich Keffer and Keffer's son, Bechtolff von Hanau—were still with him. Historians believe that Keffer and von Hanau had printed smaller books at Gutenberg House while Gutenberg concentrated on the 42-line Bible at Humbrecht House. Keffer and von Hanau had brought Gutenberg the bad news when he lost his lawsuit with Fust. These men would not likely have turned their backs on their friend.

Gutenberg still printed copies of the *Donatus*, along with other publications, such as calendars, flyers to support a Turkish crusade, and a one-page prayer. Some historians believe that Gutenberg completed another Bible, too. This edition had 36 lines to a page, making it easier to read. Gutenberg did not put his name or logo on this work. But Gutenberg's unique typeface, which came to be called D-K type, was his alone. Many also believed

A sample of text from the 36-line Bible attributed to Gutenberg

that Gutenberg printed the *Catholicon*, a 746-page religious Latin dictionary, in 1460. In the back is a colophon that most historians believe to be Gutenberg's words:

> *The noble book,* Catholicon, *in the year of our Lord's incarnation, 1460, in the mother city of Mainz of the renowned German nation . . . without help of reed, stylus or quill, but by a wonderful concord, proportion and measure of punches and formes has been printed and finished.*[4]

Trouble in Mainz

In October 1462, when Gutenberg was about 64 years old, Mainz again erupted in political chaos.

About 400 people died after a fierce battle between the citizens of Mainz and soldiers for Adolf, the Roman Catholic archbishop. Gutenberg once again left the city, along with hundreds of others. Gutenberg had criticized Adolf, and he had used his press to print propaganda against the archbishop. With no time to gather any belongings, Gutenberg abandoned his workshop.

In the spring, most Mainz citizens were invited to return to the city, but not Gutenberg. Fust and Schöffer returned to the city and began printing books for the Catholic Church. Gutenberg and 400 others were banned for life from coming within one mile (1.6 km) of the city. Gutenberg would never live in Mainz again. His house was rented to one of Adolf's supporters. Meanwhile, Gutenberg settled in Eltville, where he had fled as a teenager. He had a niece there and some patrician

Donatus Typeface

When Gutenberg first designed the typeface for the *Donatus*, he tried to imitate the handwritten look of the scribes. He even included the accent marks that scribes used to indicate short forms of words. And he had to create as many as 12 variations of some letters. This thick, rectangular type was used for all 24 editions of the *Donatus*. Gutenberg also used the same style of type for calendars he printed from year to year. Thus, the type came to be called Donatus-Kalender—D-K for short.

friends—the Bechtermünzes—whom he had known as a teenager.

With the help of the Bechtermünzes, Gutenberg established another print shop along the cobblestone streets of Eltville. Eventually, Archbishop Adolf made peace with Gutenberg, as the religious man needed printers on his side. The archbishop granted Gutenberg some money and enough grain and wine every year for a sizable household. Gutenberg was also excused from paying taxes. The terms were laid out in a letter to Gutenberg dated January 17, 1465, which bore the seal of Archbishop Adolf II von Nassau. Adolf praised this man who had devoted his life to printing:

> We . . . have recognised the agreeable and willing service which our dear, faithful Johann Gutenberg has rendered, and may and shall render in the future. . . . We shall,

The 36-line Bible

Historians debate whether Gutenberg printed the 36-line Bible. Thirty-six lines of type would require three volumes. This would use far too much paper and vellum to be cost effective for a man like Gutenberg. Some historians think that one of Gutenberg's workmen printed the 36-line Bible. They suggest that a workman could have taken the font and printed the Bible when paper became less expensive.

each and every year when we clothe our ordinary courtiers,
clothe him at the same time like one of our noblemen.[5]

All this was in exchange for Gutenberg's sworn oath that he would be loyal to the archbishop and keep his printing press available for Adolf's use.

Gutenberg's pardon also allowed him to visit Mainz without being arrested. And he did visit Mainz in 1465. There, he saw that printing was flourishing. Print shops were everywhere. And common people were purchasing more and more books. His printing press was changing the world, fulfilling his hope of giving people "wings to truth."

In 1466, Gutenberg's archrival, Johann Fust, went to Paris and died

Gutenberg's Bibles Today

As of 2007, 48 copies of the 42-line Bible exist, and 21 of them are considered to be in perfect condition. Eleven are printed on vellum, of which four are in perfect shape. The copies are spread around the world. Germany has the most copies with 12. The United States has 11 copies, and Great Britain has 8 copies. The rest are in Austria, Belgium, Denmark, France, Japan, Poland, Portugal, Russia, Spain, Switzerland, and Vatican City.

The 11 copies in the United States are in nine separate locations, including the Library of Congress in Washington DC. In 1974, the University of Texas at Austin purchased a perfect paper copy of Gutenberg's 42-line Bible for $2.4 million. During the 1920s, a New York bookseller, Gabriel Wells, purchased a damaged paper copy and sold the pages one by one. Depending on their condition, these pages now sell for $20,000 to $100,000 each.

there of the plague. Two years later, Johannes Gutenberg died without fanfare. Years later, in the margin of an obscure book, someone found a handwritten note that read: "AD 1468, on St Blasius' Day [February 3] died the honoured master Henne Ginsfleiss [Johannes Gutenberg] on whom God have mercy."[6] The hidden note would be the only record of the day Johannes Gutenberg died. It was a fitting tribute to the man who had lived most of his life in secrecy.

The Gutenberg Bible on Film

In the 2004 film *The Day After Tomorrow*, one scene shows people burning books inside the New York City Public Library in order to stay warm. One person holds one volume of the Gutenberg Bible to guard it from being burned.

Gutenberg settled in Eltville when he was banned from Mainz.

The Gutenberg Museum honors Johannes Gutenberg's life and work.

ETCHED IN HISTORY

Johannes Gutenberg was buried at
St. Francis Church at the Convent of the
Friars Minor in Mainz, Germany, in 1468. No
stone marked his grave. He was laid to rest at the
same place he had lost his printing business

13 years before. It was where a judge had ordered Gutenberg to pay Johann Fust all the money owed on two loans. Although Gutenberg was gone, his ideas and his printing methods lived on. In fact, they ballooned into a revolution of printing and the dispersal of information that spread throughout Europe.

Germany provided a strong foundation for this revolution. It had everything a good printer needed: plenty of metals, experienced calligraphers and engravers, excellent printers, wealthy investors, and at least seven printing presses. Germany dominated the printing market for years. German printers traveled everywhere, negotiating print jobs and training apprentices in other cities. In turn, these apprentices set up their own businesses.

PRINTING SPREADS THROUGH EUROPE

Every year, Johann Fust traveled to Frankfurt to sell the 42-line Bible and other books at the Frankfurt Book Fair, an event established by local booksellers. The fair quickly became one of the most important events in Europe. Printers and booksellers came from all over to sell their latest books. They also took orders for the next ones to be printed. Books were turning Frankfurt into a prosperous city.

Of course, printing spread beyond Germany, including to France and England. A print shop was established at the University of Paris-Sorbonne in 1470, and the university put in orders for published items. In 1476, William Caxton established England's first printing press in Westminster Abbey. He was England's first printer and the first person to print in English.

By 1480, only 12 years after Gutenberg's death, 122 European cities had printing presses. These presses were churning out books and printed materials in a variety of languages. Italy had 50 print shops—20 more than Germany had at that time. France, the Netherlands, Spain, Belgium, Switzerland, England, and Bohemia each had a number of presses.

Venice, Italy, was practically overrun with printers. Competition was so great that some of them

Frankfurt Book Fair

Today, the Frankfurt Book Fair in Frankfurt, Germany, is the world's largest international book fair. Representatives from publishing companies worldwide attend the five-day event. More than 7,000 exhibitors from more than 100 countries participate each year. The fair is considered the most important marketing event for new books. Participants include publishers, booksellers, illustrators, agents, librarians, authors, and other book lovers.

went out of business. Other printers, such as Aldus Manutius, came up with new ideas to keep their businesses going strong. Manutius created a new type that looked like cursive handwriting—known today as italic. Then, he printed books that would be affordable to all. These handy, pocket-sized books had soft vellum covers, similar to modern-day paperbacks. But Manutius's decision to publish in Greek was what made his business boom. Until then, no one had ever created type for the Greek alphabet. He began this venture by hiring only Greeks. These scholars, calligraphers,

Gutenberg's Press

Doctor Conradt Humery purchased Johannes Gutenberg's printing equipment 23 days after Gutenberg's death. The receipt indicates that Archbishop Adolf of Mainz required Humery to make certain promises concerning any future sale of Gutenberg's equipment:

I, Conradt Humery, doctor, make known by this letter: Whereas . . . Lord Adolf, archbishop of Mainz, had graciously permitted sundry forms, letters, instruments, tools and other things pertaining to the work of printing, which Johann Gutenberg has left after his death, and which have belonged and still belong to me, to come into my possession, therefore, I, to honour and please his Grace, did bind, and do bind myself by this document, to wit: That should I now or hereafter make use of the said forms and tools for printing, I will do so within the city of Mainz and nowhere else; that, likewise, in case I should desire to sell them and a citizen should be willing to give me as much for them as a stranger, then will and shall I give and deliver them to the resident citizen of Mainz in preference to all strangers.[1]

and engravers could speak classical Greek and knew
how to create Greek type. By the 1490s, Manutius
was producing pocket editions of Greek texts that
would make classical literature affordable to all.
He marketed *Hero and Leander*, the Greek *Psalter*, and
the works of Aristotle, Aristophanes, Thucydides,
Herodotus, and others.

Slowly and steadily, Gutenberg's printing press
was revolutionizing the world. By 1500, more than
30 years after the inventor's death, the number
of print shops had grown to 1,000. This increase
made reading materials more readily available to the
masses. Individuals owned books and were reading
and learning more than ever before in history. They
became knowledgeable in religion, science, logic,
architecture, geography, plants, animals, people,
and much more.

People who chose printing as a profession were
often successful. They ran huge establishments with
many employees. They coordinated with scholars to
publish information with the utmost accuracy. Then,
printers figured out how to market and sell their
books to a world that was energized by the art and
scholarship of the Renaissance.

PRINTING AND REVOLUTION

By 1500, more than 20 million books were in print. The printing press had already changed the way people thought about and shared information. And, just as the Catholic Church had feared, the mass production of the Bible and other religious books had taken away some of its authority.

In the early 1500s, a Catholic priest named Martin Luther studied his own copy of the Bible. He developed an alternate theology of grace that would turn the Catholic Church upside down. In 1517, Luther declared his displeasure with the Church by listing 95 topics of debate, or complaints against the Church. He wrote the complaints on a broadside, or large sheet. Then, he nailed the broadside to the door of Castle Church in Wittenberg, Germany. His list came to be called the *95 Theses*.

But Luther's broadside did not cause a spiritual revolution on its own. Someone translated Luther's *95 Theses* from Latin to German and printed copies of it. Three editions of Luther's work were printed in

Banned Books

In 1559, Pope Paul IV openly opposed certain books, particularly those written by Martin Luther. He called these books heretical, or not in agreement with the accepted beliefs of the Roman Catholic Church. He created the *Index Librorum Prohibitorum*, the "List of Prohibited Books." The list grew each year. By the time it was abolished in 1966, 4,000 books were on the list.

Martin Luther's 95 Theses was published by many printers, and his ideas spread across Europe.

three cities. Within two weeks, thousands of copies spread throughout Germany. Within a month, all of Europe knew about the *95 Theses*. Luther's ideas caused a huge uprising. Printers now devoted much of their time to printing Luther's popular writings. Between 1518 and 1519, Luther wrote 92 works that were reprinted 220 times.

For the first time in history, common people were reading and evaluating new ideas in mass-produced printed material. Those documents changed religion and unleashed what came to be called the Reformation. This era began just 62 years after Gutenberg perfected his printing press. Today, both Luther and Gutenberg are credited with sparking the Reformation. But even in the sixteenth century, Luther recognized that printing played a big part in the upheaval. He described printing as "God's highest and extremist act of grace, whereby the business of the gospel is driven forward."[2]

Incunabula

During the seventeenth century, historians came up with a Latin name for the entire group of the first printed books. They called them *incunabula*. The word means "swaddling clothes" or "infancy." It refers to books printed from movable type before 1501. Approximately 30,000 books are available in an online database, the Incunabula Short Title Catalogue.

The printing press would go on to ignite other significant events and movements, such as William Tyndale's English translation of the Bible, which was printed by Peter Schöffer. Gutenberg's press also encouraged the Enlightenment, a period from the 1600s to the late 1700s that was marked by an emphasis on reasoning. The Industrial Revolution, which started in the late 1700s, began a shift from manual labor to the use of factories and machines. It also gained momentum because of the spread of printed material. Printing would create a middle

Remembrance

Thirty-one years after Gutenberg's death, his cousin, Adam Gelthus, published a memorial to his memory at St. Francis Church: "To Johann Gensfleisch, the inventor of the art of printing and deserver of the highest honours from every nation and tongue, Adam Gelthus places [this memorial] to the immortal memory of his name. His remains rest peacefully in the church of St. Francis at Mainz."[3]

class—a people who were no longer unlearned peasants ruled by the educated elite. Ordinary people were reading and learning more. They were taking control of their own lives.

Johannes Gutenberg never received an award or an honor, nor did he receive credit during his lifetime for developing the printing press. However, his legacy was continued in every print shop that sprang up for centuries to come, with every new font, punch, matrix, or type. On every printed page, Gutenberg would be memorialized. In a way, every book would be marked with Gutenberg's name—a name now indelibly etched in history as the simple German entrepreneur who forever changed the world.

Gutenberg's 42-line Bible was his most important work.

TIMELINE

ca. 1400	1411	1414
Johannes Gutenberg is born, possibly in June, in Mainz, Germany.	Gutenberg and his family flee Mainz and go to Eltville.	Gutenberg and his family return to Mainz.

1433	1434	1439
Gutenberg's mother, Else Wirich, dies.	Gutenberg demands and receives payment of his inherited Mainz annuity.	Gutenberg partners with three craftsmen to make mirrors for Aachen pilgrims and is sued by relatives of one partner.

1419	1420	1428
Gutenberg's father, Friele Gensfleisch, dies.	Gutenberg graduates from the University of Erfurt.	Gutenberg flees Mainz due to political and economic strife and goes to Strasbourg.

1444	1448	1449
Gutenberg leaves Strasbourg. No record exists of his whereabouts for the next four years.	Gutenberg sets up a print shop in Mainz.	Gutenberg forms a partnership with Johann Fust and borrows money from him.

TIMELINE

1450	1452	1455
Gutenberg finishes printing the *Ars Grammatica*, or *Donatus*.	Gutenberg begins printing the 42-line Bible.	Gutenberg completes the pages of the 42-line Bible.

1463	1465	1468
Gutenberg leaves Mainz in October and goes to Eltville. He is banned from Mainz the following year.	Gutenberg is pardoned by the archbishop of Mainz and returns to the city for a visit.	Gutenberg dies on February 3 and is buried in Mainz.

1455	1460	1460
Gutenberg loses a lawsuit filed by Fust and surrenders his equipment and Bible pages to Fust on November 6.	Gutenberg may have finished printing a 36-line Bible and prints the *Catholicon*.	Heinrich Eggestein and Johann Mentelin print the first German version of the Bible.

1476	1500	1517
William Caxton sets up England's first printing press.	Approximately 1,000 print shops operate in 17 European countries and 245 cities; more than 20 million books are in print.	Martin Luther's *95 Theses* is printed and mass distributed, causing a spiritual revolution called the Reformation.

ESSENTIAL FACTS

DATE OF BIRTH
ca. 1400

PLACE OF BIRTH
Mainz, Germany

DATE OF DEATH
February 3, 1468

PARENTS
Friele Gensfleisch and Else Wirich

EDUCATION
University of Erfurt

MARRIAGE
none

CHILDREN
none

RESIDENCES
Mainz, Germany; Eltville, Germany; Strasbourg, France

CAREER HIGHLIGHTS

❖ Gutenberg successfully developed a working printing press.

❖ Gutenberg printed a widely popular 42-line Bible.

SOCIETAL CONTRIBUTION

Gutenberg's development of a movable type printing press allowed for the inexpensive and efficient creation of printed literature. This helped spread new ideas and educate common people. Within decades of Gutenberg's death, the dissemination of printed material gave rise to the Reformation and later led to other reforms.

CONFLICTS

After Gutenberg defaulted on a loan, Johann Fust sued the inventor for the printing press and all the work Gutenberg had so far produced. Gutenberg essentially lost his life's work to Fust. Also, conflict between the patricians and the guild members in Mainz forced Gutenberg to leave the city many times.

QUOTE

"Surely [Gutenberg] is worthy to be loaded with divine honors by all the Muses, all the arts, all the tongues of those who delight in books."—*Guillaume Fichet*

ADDITIONAL RESOURCES

SELECT BIBLIOGRAPHY

Füssel, Stephan. *Gutenberg and the Impact of Printing*. Trans. Douglas Martin. Burlington, VT: Ashgate, 2003.

Kapr, Albert. *Johann Gutenberg: The Man and His Invention*. Trans. Douglas Martin. Brookfield, VT: Ashgate, 1996.

Lienhard, John H. *How Invention Begins: Echoes of Old Voices in the Rise of New Machines*. New York: Oxford UP, 2006.

Man, John. *Gutenberg: How One Man Remade the World with Words*. New York: Wiley, 2002.

Thorpe, James. *The Gutenberg Bible: Landmark in Learning*. San Marino, CA: Huntington Library, 1999.

FURTHER READING

Beckham, Robert. *Who in the World Was the Secretive Printer? The Story of Johannes Gutenberg*. New York: Norton, 2005.

Childress, Diana. *Johannes Gutenberg and the Printing Press*. Breckenridge, CO: Twenty-First Century Books, 2007.

Meltzer, Milton. *The Printing Press*. Salt Lake City, UT: Benchmark, 2009.

Web Links

To learn more about Johannes Gutenberg, visit ABDO Publishing Company online at **www.abdopublishing.com**. Web sites about Johannes Gutenberg are featured on our Book Links page. These links are routinely monitored and updated to provide the most current information available.

Places to Visit

Gutenberg Museum
Liebfrauenplatz 5, Mainz, Germany 55116
011 49 06131 12 26 40
www.gutenberg-museum.de/?language=e
Exhibits include a reconstruction of Gutenberg's print workshop and demonstrations of how his printing press worked. The re-creation has been shown at a large number of exhibitions all over the world.

Library of Congress
Jefferson Building, 10 First Street SE, Washington, DC 20540
202-707-2905
www.loc.gov
On display is the 42-line Gutenberg Bible. Next to it is the last known copy of a handwritten Bible, possibly the copy Gutenberg used as a model for his printed Bible.

Museum of Printing History
1324 West Clay Street, Houston, TX 77019
713-522-4652
www.printingmuseum.org
The museum displays historical documents, fine art prints, and antique printing equipment. Exhibitions, lectures, and demonstrations are available to the public.

Glossary

annuity
A contract by which a person receives regular payments on an investment.

broadside
A large sheet of paper usually printed on one side and used as an advertisement or a public notice; also called a broadsheet.

bubonic plague
A contagious, sometimes fatal, disease characterized by high fever and buboes, or blisters.

calligrapher
A person skilled in the art of fine handwriting.

chase
A rectangular metal frame into which frames filled with type are locked for printing.

convent
A building occupied by a community of nuns bound by religious vows.

engraver
A person skilled in carving, cutting, or etching letters or designs into a certain material.

forge
A furnace used for heating metal.

frame
A rectangular enclosure in which type is arranged to prepare it for printing.

goldsmith
A person who makes jewelry and other articles out of gold.

guild
An association of merchants or artisans of the same trade or profession.

guilder
A gold coin once used as a basic unit of money in Germany, Austria, and the Netherlands.

liturgical
> Referring to an approved form of religious worship.

matrix
> A mold used to form impressions of type in metal blocks.

metallurgy
> The science of creating useful objects from metals.

mint
> A place where the official coins of a country are made.

monastery
> A building occupied by a community of monks bound by religious vows.

patrician
> A member of the ruling class in medieval cities of Germany and Italy.

pilgrimage
> A journey to a sacred place.

printing press
> A machine used to exert pressure on inked metal type and transfer the impressions to paper.

punch
> A tool for stamping a design into a surface.

relic
> An object from the past that has historical, religious, or personal significance.

relief
> A raised shape carved on a surface.

versal
> A large, artistically designed letter often found at the beginning of a chapter of a book.

Source Notes

Chapter 1. The Work of the Books

1. "Helmasperger's Notarial Instrument." Sect 5. *Gutenberg Digital*. 6 Jan. 2009. <http://www.gutenbergdigital.de/gudi/eframes/helma/frmnot/frmnotf.htm>.

2. Gerald Donaldson. *Books: Their History, Art, Power, Glory, Infamy and Suffering According to Their Creators, Friends and Enemies*. New York: Van Nostrand Reinhold, 1981. np.

3. "Helmasperger's Notarial Instrument." Sect 12–13. *Gutenberg Digital*. 6 Jan. 2009. <http://www.gutenbergdigital.de/gudi/eframes/helma/frmnot/frmnotf.htm>.

4. Ibid. Sect. 9.

5. James Thorpe. *The Gutenberg Bible: Landmark in Learning*. San Marino, CA: Huntington Library, 1999. 30–31.

Chapter 2. Patricians' Child
None

Chapter 3. A City Divided
None

Chapter 4. Mysterious Business

1. Albert Kapr. *Johann Gutenberg: The Man and His Invention*. Trans. Douglas Martin. Brookfield, VT: Ashgate, 1996. 55.

2. Ibid.

3. John Man. *Gutenberg: How One Man Remade the World with Words*. New York: Wiley, 2002. 59.

4. Albert Kapr. *Johann Gutenberg: The Man and His Invention*. Trans. Douglas Martin. Brookfield, VT: Ashgate, 1996. 77–78.

5. Ibid. 79.

Chapter 5. The Printing Press

1. Henri-Jean Martin. *The History and Power of Writing*. Trans. Lydia G. Cochrane. Chicago: University of Chicago Press, 1994. 217.

Source Notes Continued

Chapter 6. Catholic Connection

1. John Man. *Gutenberg: How One Man Remade the World with Words*. New York: Wiley, 2002. 152.
2. Alphonse De Lamartine. *Memories of Celebrated Characters, Vol. 2*. 2nd ed. London: Bentley, 1854. 323.
3. Ibid. 334.
4. Albert Kapr. *Johann Gutenberg: The Man and His Invention*. Trans. Douglas Martin. Brookfield, VT: Ashgate, 1996. 162.

Chapter 7. The Gutenberg Bible

1. Albert Kapr. *Johann Gutenberg: The Man and His Invention*. Trans. Douglas Martin. Brookfield, VT: Ashgate, 1996. 165.
2. Ibid.
3. Ibid. 170.
4. Ibid.

Chapter 8. Starting Over
1. John Man. *Gutenberg: How One Man Remade the World with Words*. New York: Wiley, 2002. 194.
2. William Skeen. *Early Typography*. 1872. 248. *InternetArchive*. University of Michigan. 13 Feb. 2009 <http://www.archive.org/ stream/earlytypography00skeegoog/earlytypography00skeegoog_ djvu.txt>.
3. Albert Kapr. *Johann Gutenberg: The Man and His Invention*. Trans. Douglas Martin. Brookfield, VT: Ashgate, 1996. 201.
4. Ibid. 229, 231.
5. Ibid. 259.
6. John Man. *Gutenberg: How One Man Remade the World with Words*. New York: Wiley, 2002. 213.

Chapter 9. Etched in History
1. Albert Kapr. *Johann Gutenberg: The Man and His Invention*. Trans. Douglas Martin. Brookfield, VT: Ashgate, 1996. 263–264.
2. Louis Edward Ingelhart, comp. *Press and Speech Freedoms in the World, From Antiquity until 1998: A Chronology*. Westport: Greenwood, 1998. 32.
3. Albert Kapr. *Johann Gutenberg: The Man and His Invention*. Trans. Douglas Martin. Brookfield, VT: Ashgate, 1996. 265.

INDEX

ABOUT THE AUTHOR

Sue Vander Hook has been writing and editing books for more than 15 years. Although her writing career began with several nonfiction books for adults, Sue's main focus is educational books for children and young adults. She especially enjoys writing about historical events and people who made a difference. Her published works also include a high school curriculum and several series on disease, technology, and sports. Sue lives with her family in Minnesota.

PHOTO CREDITS